From Dark to Light

From Dark to Light

Light

Ronald Dailey

Library of Congress Control Number: 2019901648
ISBN: Hardcover   978-1-7960-1541-6
                   Softcover   978-1-7960-1540-9
                   eBook   978-1-7960-1542-3

Print information available on the last page.

Rev. date: 02/13/2019

To order additional copies of this book, contact:
Xlibris
1-888-795-4274
www.Xlibris.com
Orders@Xlibris.com
790383

CONTENTS

I'm a lover of nature, above all. My favorite place to be is the Shenandoah Mountains, hiking the waterfall trails. The animals there are so much fun to photograph and be around. It is so peaceful and relaxing, so different from the city that I live in.

On rainy days that are too wet and soggy to be out adventuring in, I take up my other passion, writing poetry. Edgar Allan Poe is my favorite author and poet. I enjoy his rhyming poems like no other. He is also from Baltimore, just a short drive from where I have grown up. I try to write as he has done, in a rhyming-meter story tale. So this book is written in the style I like to read. I read my poems as I write them down.

I am an honorably discharged marine who has served four years in Hawaii. My goal as a writer is to be in an immortal book of poems next to Edgar Allan Poe.

My Poet Introduction

I can tease you with a story;
I can tease you with a rhyme,
For if you want my words to dance,
Well, jump up and get in line.

There is nothing like a story tale
With a meaning and a ring
That captures you in a special way
As you read along and sing.

So come on along my journeys
Through my sorrows and my joys
Where the words jump off the paper
And dance around like toys.

I love to make them sing and dance
As I tell a tale, you see;
There's nothing like the story tale
When they rhyme and dance for me.

So that's how I introduce myself
'Cause I'm the story man, it's true;
I'll promise to make my words to dance
And come to life for you.

The Crypt of the Forsaken

Part 1

Westminster Church, Greene and Fayette,
upon the streets in Baltimore
outside an old dark graveyard
where death is kept and stored.

Looking past the gate—this iron gate—
I leave my fears aside;
I push the gate—this creaking gate—
and prepare to step inside.

For on this night —this rainy night—
I have come to awaken death,
yes, upon this night —this rainy night—
to steal its spoken breath.

I roam inside where ghosts reside,
searching for a way to see
the tomb that holds the corridor
that will set its spirit free.

So I look around without a sound
for the tomb he sleeps within

and, into the depths, slip underground
as my hunt, it now begins.

Upon these steps in the darkest depths
I search this crypt below
when suddenly I hear a voice
in a tone that's dark and low.

Part 2

I declare, "you best beware and be wise of what you're seeking
upon your breath to awaken death in a place with spirits sleeping;
you're just a pest disturbing rest to dare knocking upon my door,
so leave my home, my death alone and return here nevermore."

"It's my choice to hear your voice," I spoke so loud and screeching,
"upon these steps in the darkened depths to know the secrets that you're keeping,
so here I'll stay, won't go away, and hereby do implore
upon this ground—forsaken ground—to come pounding upon your door."

To my surprise, before my eyes, the tomb, it started shaking;
for in this room—impending doom—his dark soul was awaking.
I sensed my fear when death was near and heard the sounding door
to see the ghost I feared the most as a mist raised from the floor.

So there I froze as death arose as I stood there freezing
to see those eyes of the dark arise, of the soul that I was seizing;
"For you have a gift, a precious gift, and therefore I awaken
upon these steps in the darkened depths, in the crypt of the forsaken."

"For I am here, my message clear, and am wise in seeking
to steal your voice—yes it's my choice—and place it in safekeeping
to see you thrive, once again alive; I release your chamber door
for your death to be awake in me and reside forevermore."

"I say to thee, just let me be and give my death respect
as for you, you have no clue this vision you detect;
so I repeat, you best retreat and close this chamber door
and leave my home, my death alone and return here nevermore!"

So there I stood on rotten wood and would not be mistaken
to come this far, the door ajar, in this crypt of the forsaken,
for on this night—this rainy night—I would not let him be
until I host his chilling ghost and awaken him in me.

To see the door, his chamber door, I took a peek inside
upon the mist—the frozen mist—to where spirits rest and hide
to see the voice—the spoken voice—of the ghost that I was cravin'
but then to see—it frightened me—was within a giant raven.

Standing ten feet tall, I heard him call, slamming his chamber door,
to see the size of those raven's eyes, repeating, "Nevermore, nevermore";
from the haunted depths, I ran up the steps from the tomb of the forsaken
to leave his home and his death alone and to never again awaken!

The Grave

It's twelve minutes past midnight,
And you best be prepared,
For you cannot be frightened
Nor eternally scared
As you look past those shadows
And those voices you hear,
Reminiscing on ghost
You forgot through the years
Sliding past home,
While so young and so brave
Yet so darkened the hole
Of the lonely man's grave;
Yes, somewhere in distance
From up under a tree,
A dark spirit shall rise,
Break loose, and be free,
Leaving behind
A soul with soiled stains,
Sealed-up, encrypted
Skeletal remains.
Two empty sockets
Will stare up at the lid,
Forced to recollect
What that lonely man did,
Imprisoned eternal
Six feet underground,
Not one rise of light,
Not one visitor found.

Yes, somewhere in the distance,
Death—chilled to the bone,
To be forever forgotten
And always alone!

The Darkened Night

Through the wilderness I bound,
Fearless and at ease,
Prowling beneath the starlight,
Peering behind the trees.

So stealth in my perfection,
For forever I am black
As so silently I probe,
Premeditate—attack!

Sniffing the forest air,
They know and are aware
Something's out there, *lurking*,
For they feel my solemn stare.

And then . . .

In a flash and fast as lightning,
Nature in resplendence,
Instantaneous young death,
Emphatic independence.

Be it now must known
As I pull the lifeless prey,
Limp and in my grasp,
I carry it away.

Soon the dust will settle,
And the sun shall again shine bright,
But a doe will walk alone today,
The end of the darkened night.

Her Octagon of Death

Building the perfect home
Between two trees,
I'm as skillful as an acrobat
With no need for trapeze,
Spinning, weaving, crafting
Every thread in place;
I need no fancy plans
For my living space.
Yes, I am a living predator,
And my home is a net;
Ask any flying insect,
And I'm sure he'll regret
'Cause if he comes through,
He had better think twice,
Or he'll soon become
My living sacrifice.
Yes, I am born toxic,
And my venom is lethal
As my trap has just caught me
A big ole beetle;
Methodically, mathematically,
I'll stroll to him
Then inject the venom
That will do him in.
And as he lay paralyzed
Yet none the wiser,
He has met the death
Of the black widow spider.

So nutritious, so delicious,
Such a succulent delight,
I'll hang him up and string him there
For later on this night;
My cunningness, my willingness, extravagance, and bite,
It's amazing how my enemies
Put up not much a fight,
Yes, forever the arachnid,
Nature's terrorist,
As I climb back up to sleep at home and blow a good night kiss!

The Soul That Had No Name

I tried bargaining with the demons
that dance inside my brain,
but they were too busy screaming
and much too wild to tame.

So they took me to graveyard
in a cold and pouring rain
and left me in a lonely tomb
with a soul that had no name.

I knew that I was victimized;
yes, I knew that I'd been played
when he opened up the gates of hell
to a place where hatred stayed.

Searching through the darkness,
sensing the echoes underground,
listening for the whispers
just beckoning to be found.

Awakening a sleeping dragon
from an ancient time of old,
showing a place where hatred bred
of caverns filled with gold.

The dragon spoke so direct,
yet the dragon spoke so true;
he said, "You listen closely,
for these words are meant for you.

"These walls are lined in gold, you see,
as far as the earth is wide,
but to search within your heart, you see,
is to know your worth inside.

"Fortune, greed, and wealth, you see,
will take you for joyful ride
but will leave you lost and all alone
in this place where the demons died."

The dragon then just faded fast
as I stood in the pouring rain,
so lost, so wet, and all alone
with a soul that had no name.

Ali's Last Goodbye

They say her name was Ali,
A teen beyond her years,
So full of class, like broken glass,
The prom queen before her peers.

But life came at her quickly
And dealt her a mighty blow
'Cause her friends were thugs,
Got her hooked on drugs,
And she just could not let go.

It was a Monday
        On a Tuesday
On a Wednesday afternoon,
        But she was so high
In late July
That she's been dead
        Since half past June.

When your mind is lost
        And jaded,
When your brain is fried
        And faded,
No matter what you do
When you have no clue
Of this precious life
You've wasted.

It was a sad day
          On a Friday
On a Sunday night in June
When the drugs and gin,
          They did her in
And took her life too soon.

Well, the doctors knew
Her life was through
When she arrived that very day,
But her family stayed,
And every night they prayed
Until that day she passed away.

It was a Saturday
          On a Sunday
On a Monday in late July
When her family knelt at her bed,
And Ali closed her eyes.

She never awoke
          From the veins she poked,
And the child inside her died;
When they laid her down to rest,
The angels wept and cried.

They say the rain came down in torrents
As the roses lay wet
          And sighed;
It was her way,
          The only way
That Ali could say
          Goodbye.

A Smile and a Child

Well, there once was a child who smiled a smile
And a child who smiled so bright,
For when he smiled that marvelous smile,
It gave everyone around delight.
For everyone around him loved his smile,
Yes, the smile that that boy had;
You see, it opened up deep feelings inside
And turned the most saddened into glad.
But he had an envious brother,
Oh so jealous, yes, was he;
Now he couldn't stand his brother's smile
And thought out a strategy.
No, he couldn't stand his brother
And the attention he would get;
Oh there would be a certain day,
A certain day, you bet.
For on that certain day—
And believe me that day came
Because after this day, this certain day,
No one would be the same—
He took his brother's favorite ball,
And he threw it oh so far,
But much to dear, dear brother's fate,
He didn't see the car.
There was a thump and then a scream
And some screeching of some wheels,
And somewhere in the distance,
Death-cold hatred feels;
But that is not what matters,
And this may sound absurd

As Tommy's cruel, cruel brother
Indulged in his last words.
And Tommy said with a smile so wide
Because he never lost his touch,
And that's why everyone around him
Loved him oh so much,
For this is what and what he said,
"Oh, Mickey, don't feel so sad,
For don't you know, my brother,
You're the best friend I've ever had.
And please tell Mom and Dad
I love and miss them so,
But I believe my time is short
And now, my friend, must go."
So he closed his little eyes,
And then he clenched his little fist,
And the cruel, cruel brother realized
Of a smile he sure would miss.

The Howling Growls

Darting in
And bolting out,
Their howling growls
Are all about.
One stops here,
Another there;
One stops death cold
And sniffs the air . . .
Underneath a gray but shallow moon,
You can hear their howling tune.
On the cusp of time
And a cold, stiff breeze,
Something's rustling amongst the leaves.
Closing in,
Pinpointed out,
The circle starts;
Oh no, look out!
The teeth, the teeth,
Those cruel and perfect teeth,
The growling, the snarling,
The teeth that stand beneath.
The hair, the hair,
And oh, and lest we least forget
Those bold red eyes that stare!
There's no way in and no way out
Trapped between without a doubt.
The biting starts; the tearing starts,
The ripping of the flesh.
And what once was and used to be
Is now what looks a mess.

For the life that feeds
Off a life that bleeds
As a howling wolf does shout!
Well, the one that feeds
At once *succeeds*,
And that's what life's about!

Sands of Time

A poem entitled, a forgotten rhyme
Of endless beginnings on borrowed time;
An hourglass flows with a heart in the middle,
But somewhere between is hidden a riddle,
A time once set—concluded, confused,
Destination unknown, mindless, defused.
"Aha," says the slithering, side-winding snake
Out in the desert with his mind awake
Where molecules of sand and the hourglass burn,
A fork in the passage but a lesson to learn,
The abundance of time and the taste of the air;
While out in the desert, no need to care,
For time in the hourglass can never look back,
Can never be borrowed or mentally lapse,
Can't be reversed or turned upside down
As the world just continues round and round.
So lost in this message, just a moment or two,
And the path of the snake, sand covered no clue,
But the fork in the passage, so bright and so clear;
Every moment in time is one to hold dear.

The Wish

With a drop of a token,
A trinket or coin,
Deception alluring,
Dark forces are joined;
So what is this
You give up on prayer . . .
For unsought or unseen, no presence is there?
I laugh to myself
As I hear the voice plea,
"I wish, I wish
Give this to me."
Be it lost weight
Or a fancy new car,
To win tons of money,
Or a trip afar.
Ahhhhhhhhhhhh,
So envision the wish
And that it is granted
And bring forth a life
So enriched and enchanted,
But behind the scenes,
So unpleasant the schemes
Of the one who holds
The token of dreams;
For unlike the one who listens to prayer,
Trust in me wish or beware,
Sir Consequence
Will come out to play,
And a wish brought forth
Will have a price to pay;

Be it ever how little,
Be it ever how small,
The token of dreams
Is held by us all.
But before you let go
And let the echo be heard,
Sometimes it is best
To say not a word.

The Silent Cry
of Death

Repentance, unforgiving,
Unknowing of how you feel,
Silence ripping the broken heart
That will never mend or heal.

No one to show you mercy,
To care and hold you tight;
Somehow you found the darkness
And shall never see the light.

Outside looking in
Of the coffin you reside,
Knowing that the life you led
Had met its end and died.

No friends, no enemies,
No words to comprehend;
Simply put, it's over now,
No soul left to defend.

Captured, yes, trapped,
All sealed up in your fate,
You tried to show the world your love,
Yet all you got was hate.

Of the Horses Fallen Down in the Snow

Under the darkest clouds of wonder,
You can hear the distant thunder
On the fields they lay asunder
Of the horses fallen down in the snow.

The heat of the cannon flashes
As the men disappear in masses;
The sway of the blade, it slashes
Of the horses fallen down in the snow.

Through the towns they rape and plunder
Upon the secret roads down under;
A general bleeds out his blunder
Wherever his heart may go.

The southern belles in weeping sashes
Lay down their loved ones' ashes
Through the blue and gray death clashes
Of the horses fallen down in the snow.

On the footpaths of the past we borrow
Of the soldiers who fought for our tomorrow;
Our hearts weep with sullen sorrow
Of the horses fallen down on the snow.

A Perfect Kind of Love

Underneath the starlit sky
When there is only you and I,
We look up at the moon and see
This moment of tranquility.

Thus, our music plays soft and low,
The fire within our hearts aglow;
We stare up at the stars and see
This moment of serenity.

And as our candles burn on through the night,
The fragrance of love we hold so tight;
We stare up at the sky and see
This moment we share in ecstasy.

Then alas, my love, my maiden fair,
This is the beautiful love we share
As we stare into the night above
Knowing we'll forever be in love.

So as we cuddle and drift off to sleep
With a silent kiss so soft and sweet,
We dream of a love as love should be,
A perfect love for eternity!

Entranced—A Shakespearean Sonnet

As she stripped there in her seductive pose,
She winked at me with a surprise and smile;
How I loved to see her without her clothes;
My heartbeat stopped, jumped, stunned for just a while.

How beautiful she was just standing there;
She knew my weakness and of my desire
As I sat there paralyzed with my stare,
Taking in her presence to admire.

Her fragrance empowered her even more;
It was so hard for me to show restraint,
Leaving me breathless so much to endure,
For my purpose here was to only paint.

Entranced as she stood there before my eyes,
Wanting her so badly was my demise.

Words

Some words we cherish wisdom;
Some words leave us with doubt;
To deprive our world of knowledge
Are the words we keep left out.

Words can be quite magical;
They can be powerful in verse;
When put together one by one,
They can rock the universe.

Words are meant to educate
For a mind to adventure and explore
Just to imagine the possibility
And hunger for so much more.

Words to me are puzzles;
Put together they sound great,
But if I could rid the world of one bad word,
I'd delete the word called "hate."

Dracula's Halloween

Witches and goblins,
vampires and pirates
are all coming down for the feast;
a princess, an angel,
a faerie, a damsel
are all well aware of the beast . . .

For tonight in their glory,
they all tell a story,
for you hear a knock at your door
when the little voices, they say
without a penny to pay,
"Trick or treat," till their lungs are so sore . . .

So the candy, it mounts
in astronomical counts
as if there were sense for the reason
as a pumpkin glows red
to awaken the dead
in just the right time of the season . . .

The night breeze is a chill
to enlighten the thrill,
for you can feel the death grip of the air
when the grim reaper, he poses
with a dozen black roses,
so willing to give and to share . . .

Yes, the children, they roam
until it's time to go home,
with ghost whispering in their heads;
as in visions and dreams,
the sweet vanilla moon beams,
casting shadows all around their beds!

Existence

Riding into a place all too familiar,
The surroundings he hasn't seen in a while,
But as he looked down
Down on the ground,
He remembered and cherished her smile . . .

High atop his mighty stallion, Rapture,
Staring down at the shadows below,
Breathing the air,
He couldn't help but stare
At the footprints left behind in the snow . . .

Then his eyes, they watched the ocean
As the waves crashed on the sea,
The desolate tune;
"So far the moon
As is her smile for me."

But he remembered her eyes
And her hunger;
He remembered her dreams
And her stare;
He remembered her thoughts and emotions
And the times they used to share.

So he patted the horse so softly
And turned him so wide in the snow
But smiled a smile of existence
Of a time not long ago.

Who Is Really the King of Beasts?

This story begins with a disgusted male lion that has been told he is not the king of beasts, that is, until he can slay a tiger—now not just any tiger, mind you, but a Siberian tiger. The lion has gathered up some animals for his long journey to Asia, the home of the Siberian tiger. This is the story of that journey.

Once upon under a midnight star,
on a dense dark jungle trail afar,
A mighty lion sang out his song
while all his followers tagged along.

This is the song the lion sung,
with the words just flowing off his tongue.
He sang this with his head held high
while his kingdom marched on by.

"For I am Lion, the king of the beasts,
the king of the beasts and then;
yes, I am Lion, the king of the beasts.
I'm king because I am."

Then the animals, they all joined in,
which made the lion smile and grin.
They sang his song real strong and loud,
which made the lion so stout and proud.

"Yes, he's the one who wears the crown,
and we animals all agree,
for he is Lion, the king of the beasts,
in charge from sea to sea.

"Keeping in line and nature in check,
this land is now his home.
For he is the lion, the king of the beasts,
and no one can take his throne.

"Yes, he is the lion, the king of the beasts,
the king of the beasts and more."

Then the animals all stop and pose
as the lion bellows out this close.

"I am the lion, the king of the beasts;
just listen to my roar."

Then the lion let out a ferocious roar,
which trembled and shook the forest floor.
And with his keen ears, he heard a sneeze;
something was hiding in the trees.

The lion was beside himself without a doubt
as he screamed and shouted out,
"Hey, you, hiding where I can't see,
your presence is needed in front of me!"

The animals couldn't believe their eyes,
for what came out was quite huge in size.

With every move, he showed his strength,
even though he was twelve feet in length.

Now the lion had to show that he had no fear,
So he said these words right loud and clear.
"What you see in back of me is surely no mirage,
for what you see, they honor me, my animal entourage."

As a batch of vultures fly on by,
the tiger boasted his reply.

"I have no time for this and that;
all I am is a big striped cat.
I heard your song, to say the least,
but I am also a magnificent beast."

The tiger went on to include,
quite intent and also rude,

"It's no wonder you have that fancy name;
the animals you rule are all but tame.
I hope you interpret this message send.
I just know you brought your best, my friend."

The lion was furious with this accusation
And said this in retaliation.

"For I am king of beasts, and I am Lion,
and with these words, you should be flying
in the other direction; now don't you see,
I resent the fact you stand up to me."

The lion said this in the dawn of light
as the two prepared for a vicious fight.

They leaped and collided with a tremendous thud,
they slipped, they tumbled into the mud.
The tiger followed through with an almighty slash
that left the lion with a horrendous gash.

The lion looked down in disbelief,
and then he grinned and showed his teeth.

"Now that was fast, very fast indeed;
you nasty tiger, you made me bleed."
He said this as he shook his head.
"This is the first time that I've bled."

The lion shrugged his shoulders as to expect
he was showing the tiger his respect.

Then the tiger went into a ravenous fit
and tore into the lion lightning quick.
Ripping and tearing, the lion fell back,
suddenly realizing he was under brutal attack.

The lion's comrades could not believe what next they heard,
for what came from the king sounded quite absurd.

"I say to you, Tiger, now quit while you're ahead;
it's not my wish to see you dead.
I'm not used to this kind of pain;
I figure this fight has not much to gain."

The lion was trying to back down gracefully,
but the tiger answered back unexpectedly.

"Now see here, Lion, this fight is a test;
we're going to fight to the finish to see who's best.
There's no backing down and no retreat;
now stand your ground and prepare to be beat."

The tiger was confident; he also felt cool,
but now the enraged lion showed why he did rule
because now the lion fought fast, and he also fought hard
and caught a startled tiger surprised and off guard.
The lion bit through skin, flesh, meat, and bone
as the tiger cried out; in pain, he did moan.

The tiger being strong, somehow he broke free
and bowed to the lion, showing dignity.
The tiger looked the lion straight into the eye,
Took a deep breath, and said this reply.

"I must say, Lion, I am rather envious
to come and find out you are quite dangerous."
Then the tiger shrugged his shoulders as to expect;
he was returning the lion with his respect.

Then the lion tackled the tiger with a tremendous thrust,
rolling him over and about, kicking up dust.
The tiger felt the pressure of the lion's jaws
as the lion felt the slashing of the tiger's claws.

They fought like this for a day and a night,
suddenly realizing they were too tired to fight.

They looked at each other and sighed a deep breath,
each of them knowing they were close to death.

Together, at once, they stood up confused,
neither backing down, both bloodied and bruised,
all of this happening under a tree of spruce
as the two came to their senses and came to a truce.

The lion spoke first underneath that great tree
as the tiger listened intently to the lion's plea.

"I am going back to my desert home;
that is where I'll continue to hold my throne.
And you there, Tiger, may you persevere;
my presence is definitely not needed here."

The tiger answered back, both proud and stern,
appreciating the lesson they both had learned.

"Yes, now, Lion, you go in peace
and feast you on the wildebeest.
The jungle is where I will roam,
where it will always be my home."

They each walked off, going their own way,
always remembering what happened that day,
the superior battle that ended with a draw
but a respect for each other and hence the law.

The lion rules the desert,
the tiger the jungle,
A truce that remains to this day.

Visions

A permanent procedure,
Transparent, although there
Are visions recollected,
Stored with special care
In a darkened space
Behind a bolt-locked door;
A mind files its memories
That only one can take the tour.

Unless the moment shared
So divine, so pure, so true
That the etching there exists
Not for one but two . . .

So . . .

This permanent museum
Forever on display,
Shadows walk the corridors,
Where wandering thoughts may stray.

So when you close your eyes
For visions lost in time
To find the melted, painted rose
Is alive and doing fine.

Now feel the frozen smile,
That warm, heartfelt surprise
As you welcome back reality
That sparkles in your eyes.

A feeling fresh, so true,
That moment shared by two
That the bloom of a new and painted rose
Was waiting there for you.

Awaiting there, you see,
Oh so patiently,
Placed in the hidden corridor,
A gift to you
From me.

The Wishing Well

To wish upon a wishing well
with a pocketful of gold,
to flip in my dark request
where souls are bought and sold.

Staring down at my reflection,
which is staring back at me,
I toss down my golden fortune,
wondering what my wish will be.

Upon the ripples in the water,
I glance at the sky above,
knowing so deep within my heart
I wish to know and love.

As doves fly by, I wonder why
as if I didn't have a clue
to know upon another's heart
and to wish she'll love me too.

And to this day, so far away,
in the distance that I see
to join two hearts so far apart
and to wish she was with me.

To wish upon a wishing well,
to know of a love like none before,
to know of joy and happiness,
and to wish for nevermore!

For If You Leave, Should I Not Know?

Shall not, want not, need not care;
   I always knew that love was there,
      For when she kissed me once and twice,
      Well, I thought I was in paradise.
      But hence, she left—
            And did let go
          But never ever let me know.
Shall not, want not, need not care;
      Yes, she did; she left me there.
But she came back some time gone,
      Came on back upon my lawn,
Told me how she loved and missed me so
      And should have never let me go.
Shall not, want not, need not care;
She never knew that love was there,
      For I tell you this as this is no lie,
I turned my back and said goodbye.
Shall not, want not, need not care;
      Yes, I did, I left her there;
      You ask me why and this and then?
I tell you I shall never hurt like that again!

Drench Me in Your Glory

She cried her last tear today
    While standing by the sea;
  It dropped into an ocean wave,
Never hearing her sighing plea.
  So out into the ocean depths,
The tear, it swam away,
    Never listening to another lie
Or the words he had to say.
So into the depths of the ocean deep,
    The tear, it disappeared,
Awaiting until her silent plea
    So suddenly reappeared.
The words of encouragement
    Of love and strong devotion,
    Of how beautiful her heart was,
     The sense of such emotion,
    It started as a ripple,
     A circle in the tide
      From up under the ocean depths.
The tear began to ride;
  It was picking up momentum
    Each and every day;
  Widespread across the ocean,
    A new love would have his way.
    People took in notice
     And left the beach in fright
As the tear, it came ashore,

Crashing in the night,
But the lady stood there holding him
In her life's new story,
And the storm, it just passed them by
Then drenched them in her glory.

My School Day Adventure

I knew I'd be late for school one day
With my books and pack in tow
And decided to take the nature's path,
So off adventuring I would go.

Right away, I heard a croaking frog;
That was such a surprise to me,
So I ran on down to the pond
In a hope that I could see

Him upon a lily pad
Or chasing a wayward fly,
Maybe just sitting upon a log
Underneath a clear blue sky.

Yet as I came upon the pond,
The frog, it jumped and splashed,
But all I saw was a ripple ring,
And all my hopes had crashed.

But as I looked across the way,
I couldn't help but see
A little, tiny baby fawn
Just staring back at me.

His ears were straight and pointy
And were moving all around,
Yet I was so silently frozen,
For I dare not make a sound.

We seemed fascinated with each other
As we both stood there on that day;
Reminiscing on my adventure,
That will never go away.

The Peekaboo Squirrel

I love walking in the woods,
Exploring down the trail,
Admiring this baby squirrel
Who's wagging his little tail.

He's ever so cute and lively
As he's climbing up a tree
And decides to play a little game
Of hide-and-seek with me

He ducks into a tiny hole
And suddenly disappears,
But right before my very eyes,
He quickly reappears.

Looking out and all around
And staring back at me,
Startled by my presence there,
He hides back in the tree.

He's playing a game of peekaboo
As he keeps peeking out and in;
Then I continue on down the trail,
Just a-smiling with a grin.

Pickles, the Dancing Grizzly Bear

Hi, I'm Pickles, the bacon-eating grizzly bear
'Cause I don't like salmon
Or an occasional hare;
Yeah, I like my bacon
From a boar or a pig.
Then I get up and do the
Grizzly bear jig;
Then I go dancing
Through the forest trees.
I don't need any honey
'Cause I don't mess with the bees.
In the springtime and the summer,
You'll find me down by the lake
Stealing me some bacon
From the charcoal bake;
Then I come up dancing
With the sticks that I twirl
As the owl shakes his head,
And I twist with the squirrel.
I remember the day
The possum called me a punk
'Cause I was disco dancing
With the fox and the skunk.
Sometimes I mix it up
With some bacon and cheese;
I don't go chasing rabbits
'Cause they are loaded with fleas.

I got a hidden stash of bacon
That crashed on a plane;
There's nothing like a fancy snack
To get out of the rain.
So if you're ever in my neighborhood,
Bring some bacon to share;
Then you can come dance with Pickles,
The bacon eating grizzly bear.

Sniffles

Sniffles, the sneezing spider,
Housed up in the garlic vault,
Sneezed and sniffled all day long
Or whenever she smelled the salt.

So she climbed to the highest window
And caught a late-night breeze
When a slow and traveling tortoise
Heard the spider sneeze.

But the breeze, it was so swift
And blew her right on by,
So the slow and disgusted tortoise
Had to settle for a wayward fly.

So she climbed up into a steeple
And rested up in the bell,
And does she sneeze anymore?
Well, no one can hear to tell!

The Tale of the Four Trophies

We all know about the stories hunters come home with after a night in the woods; ever wonder if those stories are true? Well, here is a little rendition that backfires on an old-timer who has been bragging about his excursions over the years. To make matters worse, a lot of his friends are in his trophy room when one of his stuffed creatures comes to life and tells how it really happened.

Ned, who is Jack's friend, starts off the conversation. "Wow, Jack," Ned says excitedly, "I often wonder what it must have been like out there hunting these marvelous animals. You've really got yourself quite a collection. I am surely envious of your travels and your tales." Jack, who is the owner of the trophy room, just smiles at his group of friends as he lights his cigar.

Then Alice, all of a sudden, jumps out of her chair, screaming, jumping, and pointing at the polar bear, which has miraculously come to life. Then the bear says while blocking the gun rack at the same time,

"Killed the bear while charging from the bush?
Come on, Jack, you know that that is false.
If it weren't for the nature guides,
you would still be lost."

All Jack's friends look astonished by this ordeal as Jack just says,
"But . . ."
Then Jack's friend Tony says, "I think the moose wants to talk."
And sure enough, even though mounted on the wall, the moose shakes
off some dust and replies,

"Hey, guys, I'm back, and I got myself a moose.
Jack, you don't even know what's real.
You bought me at a yard sale
'Cause you knew I was a steal."

And Jack once again says, "But . . ."
Then simultaneously, the four of them turn to the white tiger, who indeed
also has something to say.

"The tiger mauled and scratched me.
Jack, your friends are dense.
You really know how you got that scar
When you fell down off that fence."

Jack could only muster a very quiet "but."
Then as surely as you know it, the lion is next.

"He was really hunting zebra
As I was hiding in a tree,
But his shot was so far off
He accidentally shot me.
And Jack, he couldn't believe it.
You should have seen his eyes
When the ranger had to show him
His blessing in disguise.
Unfortunately, I was the first

Of his almighty tales;
And if lying was a crime,
Ole Jack would be in jail."

And with that, the animals go back to being stuffed trophies again,
but Jack's friends are surely shocked at what they have heard.

And the moral of this story is
Don't always believe a hunter;
Although some tales are true,
They are often exaggerated
And not always on cue.

Snow

You hear of its arrival
But cannot wait to see
The white and dancing crystals
That are so beautiful to me,
Yes, looking out my window,
Smearing the moisture on the glass,
Hoping to get a blizzard
So there will be no class.
Thinking of tomorrow,
My world hidden from the sun,
A god made frozen tundra
For children to have fun.
Maybe I'll build a snowman
Or track a deer down by the stream;
Just imagine the possibilities
As I fall to sleep and dream
But only to awaken
Feeling like a fool,
Listening to the weatherman
Who said there'd be no school.
Looking out my window,
The sun is shining bright;
Not one white and dancing crystal
Is anywhere in sight,
So much predicting and analysis
As off to school I go,
Hoping for another day
When I will see the snow.

An Ode to ye Ole Stock Market

It was a day—
    Oh, what a day—
When the market crashed
    And burned;
Oh, what a day,
    Oh, such a day
That lesson that I learned.

The feds raised the
    Interest rates,
And I thought it was a joke
Until I looked into my account
And saw that I was broke!

The politicians are laughing;
They think it's really funny,
Buying all those lavish gifts
They stole with all my money!

The Tale of a Certain Worker

There is this certain worker—
We will call him Worker 1—
Who seems to think his workday
Is nothing but games and fun,
But when it comes to real work,
He doesn't have a clue
Because he always leaves his workload
For certain Worker 2.
Now certain Worker 2
Is busy as can be
And never has time to complain and whine
Like certain Worker 3.
I am tired of certain people
Who just show up for a check
And have made a certain workforce
Become a certain wreck.
For those of you afraid to work,
I know a certain cure;
I don't want to have to show you,
But there's the freaking door!

A Vision in the Dark

Outside, the wind was growling,
yet the house, it stood so still
you could have heard a fainted whisper
echo off the windowsill;
it gave an eerie feeling
as she lay there in her sleep,
so suddenly becoming wide awake
in a dream so dark and deep.
she had this clouded vision,
trying to make sense of what would be,
unknowing the darkened circumstance
of what her dream would see . . .

She found herself confined,
restrained, and shackled down,
lying in an open crypt
in a see-through silken gown;
her breathing began to escalate,
but no beat was within her heart.
seemingly, a beginning came to an end,
yet a finish had begun to start . . .
then the voice, it came to her
in a tone so dark and grim,
beckoning through the candlelight
forewarned of the night of sin . . .

"Oh, let me be your vampire,
your demon in masquerade

to come and give you pleasure,
to be the queen of my parade.

"Yes, the queen of dark seduction,
my princess for my own,
to live the night immortal
in the darkness where we'll roam.

"Yes, let me be your vampire,
your demon for all time,
finding you so beautiful,
knowing forever you'll be mine."

So then the voice, it faded
as she awakened from her dream;
filled with a chilled sensation,
she couldn't help but scream.
outside, the wind was growling,
yet the house, it stood so still
as the lady lay in her silken gown
with a smile that was poised to kill.

The Visitor in the Night

I am the lord of all vampires
In the full darkness of sin,
Peering into your window
With a bone-chilling grin;
Your eyes catch my stare
As so silent you scream,
Realizing your nightmare
Is no illusion or dream.
I slip past your window
And walk up to your bed
As evil, wicked thoughts
Protrude through your head;
You, the virgin in white,
Awake in the night
As the dark lord of romance
Has you now in his sight.
With the click of his fingers
And the loss of your bra,
You whisper my name,
The name *Dracula*,
And you listen to me
Lie back as I say,
"I come to you now
To take you forever away."
Without even thinking,
You throw back your hair;
In a flash of an instant,
Like a magnet, I'm there,

This moment in time,
This evil you see,
Trapped forever in nightmare
Alone here with me!

Satan Bear

Introduction

On the outskirts of a village some time ago, a small but defensible group of people believed to be of Indian descent were faced with a crisis that had suddenly come into their lives. While out tending the fields where they planted such crops as corn, wheat, and other fine vegetables, something had tragically gone wrong, for two of their people were brutally attacked and killed in the outer edge of the plantation by the foliage that preceded the forest. Unfortunately, this was not the first time an incident like this had occurred over the course of about four months. Indeed, the village had lost six members due to these cruel and inhumane types of slayings.

But it wasn't like the people of this commune didn't know what was happening, quite the contrary, I should say, for what was killing the members of their people wasn't leaving as they had once hoped. It was staying and feasting on them, living just outside the limits of their section of the world. In fact, they had given this hideous beast a name. They had called him Satan the Bear.

The leaders of the tribe then decided what to do about Satan, much to the disbelief of the people, who in general thought it would be best to move out of the area and away from Satan. The head chief instead got his best warriors to set out and kill the bear. This, in turn, caused a great deal of emotion and tension among the people; but once informed of the strategy and the belief that Satan would follow, all agreed he must be killed. This was their story of what happened the day they sought Satan the Bear.

The Poem

On edge, determined,
At the rise of first light,
Set forth, unfazed,
And prepared to fight!

Twenty men, unequaled,
Armed with spears and knives,
To take and dispose
Where the evil does thrive.

Going after Satan,
You see, this Satan's a bear
Believed to live in this cave
And to intrude to their despair.

Yes, this darkened cave,
And this cave, it is deep,
For Satan the Bear
Stands over ten feet!

Now this Satan kills men,
And these men were once tough,
But the time has come,
For enough is enough!

Now the warriors sang,
And in singing they said

That Satan the Bear
Was better off dead.

Outside of this cave,
The entrance was mud,
But surrounding this cave
Were rocks caked in blood.

Once inside of this cave,
They saw the skulls of men;
Yes, this was surely
The Satan's den.

As they went in this cave,
This cave from inside,
Every man wondered
Where this Satan might hide.

Now Satan was waiting
And waiting in there
As he stood in waiting
Without an intolerant stare.

The men held their fire,
And the fire did flare,
And then they saw the red eyes
Of that demented old bear.

Now that Satan came forward,
For he came forward hell bound;
Yes, he was truly crazed
In this cave underground.

Now the battle had started,
A one-bear stampede;
Oh, how they misjudged him,
Oh how indeed.

This Satan the Bear
Started ripping and tearing,
Just overpowering the men,
Who were dropping and swearing.

Though the men came in numbers,
And yes, their numbers were great,
The bear kept on charging
And sealing their fate.

Certainly and one by one,
Close behind and one and all,
Their numbers depleted;
They began to fall.

Until one certain boy
Who wasn't able to start
Tossed an eagle-eyed spear
Right through that bear's heart.

Now that Satan looked up;
Yes, he looked up, amazed
And through his red eyes,
Although they were dazed.

His days were through,
And he took his last breath

As that one little boy
Blew him the kiss of his death.

Now the head chief had said
Little boys should not go.
But who did deal Satan
His mighty death blow?

The time had passed
As that little boy said,
"Twenty men are down,
But hey, I'm not dead."
Then he finished by saying,
"Sometimes thoughts can deceive
When others dispute
What one can achieve!"

Yes, that one little boy,
He knew in his mind
That somehow he'd kill Satan;
He knew the whole time.

If you follow a leader,
Be it second or last in line,
Always remember
You're a step behind.

So I say in closing
Good luck and take heed.
Standing in line?
Step forward—proceed!

Abandoned

Please don't leave me stranded,
Abandoned, all alone,
For I'm just a li'l puppy
In search of a loving home.

I'll promise to keep you happy,
I'll lick, I'll love, I'll play;
You'll never know a love like mine
That you will cherish every day.

I'll bark at bad intruders;
I'll bark when cars go by,
But please don't leave me stranded,
For without you I will die.

For when you come home from work,
I'll wag my little tail;
I'm willing to learn brand-new tricks;
I'll even get your mail.

So please don't leave me stranded;
Don't leave me here today,
For I won't be here tomorrow
When you turn and walk away.

Yeah, I'm just a li'l puppy,
So lost and all alone,
Abandoned and unwanted,
Without a loving home.

Dark Places

I have been to dark places,
Seen sinister faces;
I have even fine-dined with a cat,
But in the midst of it all,
I somehow stood tall
And became one with the night as a bat.

I have been to dark places,
Seen sinister faces;
I have even sailed the loneliest sea,
But in the midst of it all,
I somehow stood tall
And realized the night was for me.

I have been to dark places,
Seen sinister faces;
I have even danced in life all alone,
But in the midst of it all,
I somehow stood tall
And took on the night as my home.

As the dark voices, they say
So far and away,
When the reaper comes calling for me,
No more words will I say,
No more light of the day,
And forever in darkness I'll be.

Yes, I have been to dark places,
Seen sinister faces,
And realized the path I do roam
For the darkness to be
Entwined forever with me
And forever to be all alone.

Death Guard

I am the soul survivor
As I trespass on through time,
Materialized evolution
Like a sentinel defined,
Standing guard over passages
So dark they bear no light,
Peering as they rest so peacefully,
Unknowing of their helpless plight—
Soldiers lost on battlefields
Or pirates lost at sea,
I am the ghost that stands this post
As grim as that may be;
Yes, their death, it does surround me
As in life they stood so brave,
Trading honor for an unjust cause
So deep down in their graves—
But their death, it does hold valor,
And their deeds are not yet done,
To fight on the final battlefield
When they join the force as one!
They shall arise from their death, awaken
As their spirits as one unite
To march in war just as before
And their souls as one ignite . . .
Comrades on the warpath,
With dragon's heart they'll fly,
Resurrected in defiance
To right their fight to die;

Their numbers insurmountable,
No force shall know their fate,
To fight the fight until it ends
And to rid the world its hate!

Her Dark Kept Secrets

Decisions, conditions with infinite visions
Of life and our destiny,
Creating suspicions subtracting additions
By the sound of her thundering seas.

From the echoes from the deep that transpire
And as a volcano erupts through the night,
Hiding the mysteries that consume us
That she will protect with all of her might.

Be it the sun or the moon or the stars high above
From the sands of the desert and oceans,
Her secrets are hidden, yes, strictly forbidden,
Dusted away through the times of erosion.

Her disasters cause mayhem and fury
As the people take heed, and they flee
When the hurricane storms up the coast
With the name that she boasts,
So violent through the eye that she sees.

Her eyes are her pools and her rivers;
Her veins are her creeks and her streams
As she lies wide awake with every breath that we take,
Confined in the midst of her dreams.

Her heartbeat is the life deep within us
As a breeze kisses the leaves through the trees,
For if you step in too close with the chill of her ghost,
You'll succumb to her death by disease.

She gives us the power to thrive and devour,
To discover her prophecies
But to never dissever, not now or forever,
From the depth of her thundering seas.

So don't ever meander in searching
For the meaning of life that we seek
Because you'll be left all alone,
Just a pile full of bones,
With the secrets forever she'll keep.

The Warrior

On the footpaths of the battlefield
Where terrorists are grown,
I defend our nation's freedom
In a mind-set of my own.
Many a night I ask myself,
As my comrades smell defeat,
It seems we lose at least one a day
As red blood spills on the streets.
But inside I'm dignified
And glorified it be;
You can't take away my selfish pride
That boils inside of me.
Out here on this battlefield,
I take in all that I see,
The nation that I fight for
And the enemy that flees.
Yes, the strong heart in the homeland
That sent me so far away,
I search the lonely stars at night
And the coming of a brand-new day.
Yeah, someday this will end,
This battle that I fight,
The warrior that I have now become
With knowledge as my sight.
I can feel the enemy;
I can feel his hate.
In this world that I exist,
There cannot be one mistake.
I know you look upon me;
I feel your eyes afar,

Thrown into the fire
With a sealed lid upon the jar.
But a warrior will make it through
Unrelentingly and no shame to speak,
Knowing he fought this battle
For the pretenders and the weak.

The Friend Request

Last night, I had a friend request
But much to my surprise,
For I found it quite unusual;
It was the devil in disguise.

He came dressed up as the joker
With a reaper cloaked in black,
Surrounded by a pack of wolves,
Poised, ready to attack!

Now I had a card up my sleeve
From earlier that day;
Yes, I had a card up my sleeve
That I could not wait to play.

For earlier that day, you see,
I had a friend request, it's true;
It came from my Lord, Jesus Christ,
Who said, "I'd fight for you."

Now Satan was beside himself
As the reaper sat and cried;
The wolves, they yelped and ran away,
The friend request denied.

Satan will come in many forms
To sway and steal your soul,
But when you have a friend in Jesus,
He will never gain control.

Secrets Kept

So many secrets go untold
And so many secrets kept,
But there is a secret I was told
And never will forget.
This tale is of two lovers
Who met on a beach one night
And who thought it best or other
That together just seemed right.
They could be seen each night and every night,
Or so that I was told,
Walking along hand in hand,
Be it warm or be it cold.
So many secrets go untold
And so many secrets kept,
But there was a night—oh, what a night—
When the man, he overslept.
Now the lady, she held dear
That secret I was told,
For on that night—oh, what a night—
She wept on her heart of gold.
Now she didn't see the tide
As the ocean, it did swell,
For it came in so tenaciously
And took the weeping belle.
The man came back the very next night
As an albatross did sing,
Carrying a secret in his sack,
For inside was a diamond ring.
Yes, he is there every night
Just standing by the sea,

Waiting for his maiden to come back,
Although she'll never be.
No one has the heart to tell him
Of this secret that we keep;
Somehow we see it the penalty
For the night he stayed asleep.

My Phone Call from Heaven

I got a dozen instant messages
And a dozen unknown calls;
Why do I even bother?
It's like talking to the walls.
I'm the only one who worries
With stress too much to bear;
My life's just one big burden,
And it just does not seem fair
'Cause no one ever listens.
Yeah, no one seems to care.
There is no God in heaven;
He never answers my prayers.
I wish I had a direct line
To heaven, don't you see?
Then perhaps He'd listen
And get in touch with me.

So one day I went out driving,
Fed up to get away,
To ride up to the mountains,
Just to spend the day
Driving up the curvy, windy road;
Then I looked up in the sky
As the clouds turned into angels
With their wings open to fly.

Then much to my surprise,
My phone began to ring
As my speakers opened up,
And I heard the angels sing.

"You say that no one listens,
And no one seems to care,
But there is a God in heaven,
Although HHhhhe can't answer all your prayers.

"Just keep that love within your heart
And never let it die;
Then you'll be with us one day,
Just flying through the sky.

"So don't give up on Jesus;
He knows that you are there.
You think that He don't listen,
And you think that He don't care.

"But there is a God in heaven
With all His love to share;
He'll never turn His back on you
If you keep your faith in prayer.

"So keep that heart wide open."
As I looked right up to see
My mother as an angel
Flying right by me.

Then the sky turned into a waterfall
That so suddenly just appeared,
Yet the angels kept on singing,
So beautiful to my ears.

You might not think He listens;
You might not think He cares,
But there is a God in heaven,
And He's just answered all my prayers.

The Story Man

So you want to hear a rhyme
Forgotten in time
That's hidden in a special place
In a box of mine,
Stored in a closet
Behind a closed, locked door
Down in a dark cellar
Buried in a dirt floor;
For as you see, this poem to me
Was never to be seen or read
And to keep it stored and locked away
Until the day that I am dead.
It was given to me
And meant to be close,
For it was given to me
By a spirit or ghost.
I cannot recall or remember why;
He just told me to hold it till the day I die.

This tale is of the story man
Who could tell a tale so well,
For the spirit told me—
Oh yes, he told me—
That he came from the depths of hell.

The spirit told me—
Oh yes, he told me—
Of these stories he could tell,
For his tales can put you in a trance,
Underneath his cold dark spell.

So this tale is of the story man
Who seeks the secrets that you keep,
For once he slips into your mind,
He'll be the dreams within your sleep.

He is called the Dark Invader,
The Intruder from Deep Within
Who will stop the beat inside your heart
And curse it in wicked sin.

There is no escape from the story man
Or the words he has to tell;
He is just out and about, leaving no doubt
Through the demon's path through hell.

You can see those under his power
Who are lost and so confused,
Befuddled in puzzles through all of their struggles,
And covered in his tattoos.

So the story man has escaped his box,
And with that, there's no mistake;
He steals the love that's within your heart
And replaces it with hate.

His disease, it is contagious
And its spread both far and wide,
For the box that held the story man
Is where Satan hid inside.

If you think that you're invincible,
That you're safe and out of view,
Remember until your fate's immortalized
The story man is after you!

Friends

Can friends indulge in a ravenous
Kiss that will make the roses bloom?
Can friends indulge in a night of love
That will melt the snow in June?

Can friends look each other in the eyes
That can fill a mind with wonder?
Can friends tingle each other with surprise
That can make a heartbeat thunder?

Can friends stay the night underneath the stars
And cuddle and talk and play?
Can friends make the hours pass away
Until the light of the newfound day?

Can friends stay friends when they are in love
Like a love that they never knew?
Can friends stay friends when they define a love
With a love that's so deep and true?

Can friends be friends
When they fall in love
And reminisce on the times they share?
Can friends stay friends
When they drift apart
Yet wish that they were there?

The Wisdom Tree

There was a tiny dragon
That stood one inch high
And thought he was invincible
Flying across the sky.

Everywhere he went
He left a trail of fire
As everyone he knew called him
The blazing flier.

He flew across the forest,
He flew across the lake,
He flew across the ocean,
Which was a big mistake.

Because he tired out
And then he couldn't see
Then crashed in the middle
Of the wisdom tree.

Everyone had told him
About the smoke in the sky;
"Be careful of what you do,
Or one day you'll die."

But he knew it all;
He was crazy as can be
And never wanted the knowledge
From the wisdom tree.

The Story Tale

I wish I could write a story tale
Where the words just dance and flow;
Imagine how magical that would be
Like Edgar Allan Poe.

Creating tales and fantasies
Of new worlds to explore,
To make the words just dance and rhyme
Like no one else before.

Yeah, I wish I could write a story tale
Where the words just jump and ring
And to make the tale come to life
As you read along and sing.

There is nothing like the story tale
That can take you back in time
With endless possibilities
In the perfect type of rhyme.

Edgar was the master
Who lived and slammed the door,
Yet they say there is an evil man
Who can write like none before!

There's nothing like the story tale;
It's like music to your ears.
Now that's the kind of poetry
That lasts for years and years.

The Forest in the Dark

I love to look up at the magical sky,
At the way the stars sparkle and glow;
Oh, the way the moon reflects on the lake,
It's quite a spectacular show.

There's nothing like being in the woods in the dark,
Captured by the scents and the views
As the campfire dances alone in the night,
And the shadows pass by in review.

The midnight air so cool and refreshed
And the sounds of brooks and the streams
As the clouds pass over the mountains
In the distance of mystical dreams.

The call of the owl that echoes,
The howl of the wolf in the dark,
The scurrying of the tiniest creatures
Are the melodious beats of the heart.

There's nothing like the beauty of the woods in the night
As I stare into the dark high above
To fall asleep upon the ground that I rest,
Surrounded by the peace that I love.

My Childhood Teaching Place

I was always staring out the window
When the teachers taught at school;
Bored to death, I couldn't catch a break
Being caught feeling like a fool.

I couldn't wait for the class to end
And run down to the woods,
For that's the place I would race
And feel I understood.

Nature just amazes me,
Running through the trails and trees
Not far from home yet all alone,
My playground without keys.

I used to scream out like an Indian
Where my imagination could just soar,
Pretending I was Geronimo
On a painted horse for war.

I couldn't wait to see the reservoir
Where I hid a raft to ride,
To cross over to my tepee tent
Just a few strokes to the other side.

It's the place where I belonged;
Out in the forest, I was me.
The woods taught me more that I cared to know,
With no teachers in view to see.

Candle, Candle

Candle, candle burning bright,
Awake and waving through the night,
Where all the weakest souls unite
That crave the reaper's appetite.

Candle, candle burning bright,
Awake and thriving through the night
From those who awake in death to see,
To take the first breath of destiny.

Candle, candle burning bright,
Awake and flaming through the night
To hear the spirits so loud and clear
For when the vision of your ghost appear.

Candle, candle burning dim,
Darkened ashes that look so grim,
For as the new day is fresh and born
Of those we lost and have to mourn.

His Dark Embrace

I await you in the darkness,
In the still breath of the night,
Through the cool and seductive atmosphere
While the moon is shining bright.
Dark spirits shall surround us
As the reaper watches time;
It won't be long now, my dear.
In mere moments, you'll be mine
As you trespass across the graveyard
Grieving of love gone by.
You fail to see a lone bat
Vanish right before your eyes;
In a flash, flesh bit an instant.
You stare at me and gasp
As I whisper in your ear,
"How long can forever last?"
So as I hold you oh so close
In this, our dark embrace,
I shall return you to your bed at home
With a forbidden smile upon my face.
Yet as I leave, for I must, dearest,
I leave a rose pinned to your dress
As I vanish as before;
Of our sins we can't confess.

For when you awaken to a brand-new day,
Standing so perfect in pose,
The mirror's reflection upon you sees
Just a beautiful dress and rose.

My Darling, My Darling, My Baby

As I wake up on this very first
morning without you,
I stare up at the beautiful sky
in nothing but wonder.
How has our world turned so vicious?
How has our world turned so cruel?
Why has our country turned its back on us?
And why am I alone without you?
You were everything to me;
You were my
Jeanie,
My Tinker Bell,
My four-leaf clover,
My merry Christmas
And happy New Year
On the Fourth of July,
In the middle of Valentine's Day,
Every day of the year.
As I scream, you're gone,
Taken away by an illegal.

My darling, my darling, my baby.
My darling, my darling, my girl,
Don't you know you're driving me crazy
Now that you're out of my world?

My darling, my darling, my princess.
My darling, my darling, my heart,
Don't you know you'll always be with me,
Even though that we're so far apart?

My darling, my darling, my angel.
My darling, my darling, my soul,
Don't you know that I always will love you
In this world that's gone out of control?

As I stare up into the heavens
Through the mist in my eyes as I cry,
I love you, my darling angel,
And I'll miss you till the day that I die.

CPSIA information can be obtained
at www.ICGtesting.com
Printed in the USA
BVHW071400210219
540828BV00005B/70/P

9 781796 015416